ISBN2 9798772439586

Cover and design created using Canva
Chakra images by Serena King

Printed in Canada

Visit www.andid.ca

Introduction

Allow me to introduce myself and tell you why I have created The Joy Journey and this 28-day journal.

I was born on January 1st, 1965 - News Years' day! My beautiful parents named me Andrea Joy. In Judaism, it is also a tradition to be given a Jewish name, in my case, Aviva - which translates to Spring. So while I was growing up, I thought I was special. No more special than all of us, really, but for me, with a middle name like Spring Joy, a birthday on new years day, and a culture of people who have survived persecution time and time again left me with a particular impression of myself at a young age.

Mostly I feel this has served me well in life. Not only as encouragement to stand firm in my beliefs but also to strive for greatness, understanding, and knowledge.

I have always been a seeker since a small child. I have early memories of contemplating the meaning of life; where do we come from? Where do we go when we die.? Are there other lifeforms? What is out there in the deep darkness of the sky, beyond the stars and galaxies?

These questions and more have been at the core of many of my choices along my path. It is the primary reason I was attracted to Yoga and Eastern Traditions at an early age. Not only was it a path to better understand me and my connection to God and the Universe, but also as a tool for exploring the Science of myself as a human being.

I went to a pretty liberal high school in the early '80s and was introduced to Yoga by one of my English teachers. Since I was ten, I had already been taking dancing lessons, so Yoga just felt very natural and comforting to me. Plus, I was very attracted to the substantial spiritual element. I was hooked and still am!

I have always been interested in the arts. I started writing songs when I was 15 and was heavily involved in the theatre department in high school. I decided I wanted to go into acting and got into the Theatre Arts program in University, but I soon found out that it was not nearly as easy as I thought, and University was not my jam, so I left after the first year. At 21, I taught myself how to play guitar and continued to write songs. When I returned from a year of travelling at 24, I decided to get into music, started my first band, and my pursuit of becoming a rock star began! I must admit I did pretty good in the Toronto Music Scene in the early 90's and then again in the early 2000's.

If we can feel joy for even
30 seconds in our day
we are still making
a difference
in our life.

Music, however, was not a career I could count on, and I figured I should have a job or skill I could fall back on if I didn't "make it." So in 1991, I went back to school to become a massage therapist. I always had a natural inclination to healing and inherited my late father's beautiful soft hands. In addition, I've always loved helping people when they were not feeling well. So this career path felt right. I graduated from Sutherland Chan School of Massage Therapy in 1991.

In 1997 I was introduced to Vipassana (Insight-based) meditation. It was also the year I began teaching Yoga. Yoga and Meditation have been and continue to be some of the most profound and joy-filled expressions of my life.

I remember the day I sat with my Sangha (meditation group) while listening to the Dharma (teachings) taught by my first meditation teacher, Beverly Yates in Toronto, thinking to myself. "Boy, I want to do this one day! I, too, want to teach people about waking up and cultivating compassion and kindness."

All this brings me to the present moment.
My ultimate goal has been to help others in healing and facilitate them to know themselves better. To empower, inspire, lift, spread light, and most importantly, to know Joy. I have a natural and innate ability of intuition and empathy, which has served me well in my 30-year practise as an Integrative Body Therapist and what I like to call a Soul Coach.

I created this book for you as a means for you to record your 28 Day Journey to Joy. Each day I have asked you to reflect on your practice by asking you a question or two. In addition, feel free to record other personal experiences as a means of reflection and growth.

I wish and intend that you
understand the nature of your TRUE SELF and experience life's joys daily.

In peace and friendship;
Andi D.

The
Joy
Journey

To know Joy
Fully and completely
is to keep coming back to
– this moment –
time and time again

What I Know For Sure

I know that stress is, hands down, one of the primary causes of pain and illness. In addition, when the brain is in considerable amounts of continuous - fight, flight freeze, - our natural immune system begins to break down, making us susceptible to various syndromes and conditions.

We live in a culture curated on consumerism, financial gain, vanity and fear. Social Media consumes us. We spend more and more time on our devices than we do simply talking with one another, getting outside for exercise, reading a book or doing a puzzle. I see how this lifestyle affects people every single day. This is especially prevalent in today's youth.

As an alternative health care provider, I work with people suffering in many different ways. Acquired brain injuries, concussions, migraines, chronic pain, chronic stress, chronic fatigue, anxiety, depression, and almost all of these include grinding and clenching of the teeth and jaw.

In 30 years of practice professionally and personally, what I know for sure is; healing will not come from me and me alone. If all of a person's recovery is in my hands, and my hands alone, chances are that client will not recover fully. It must be a joint effort.

Those that meet me halfway, are willing to be honest (I am known for being straight up and to the point, in a kind and loving way!) and do the homework I give them, are the ones that heal more successfully. Those who understand healing is a mind, body, energy connection and do what it takes to tether this union are the ones who live a more fulfilling life with much less stress and suffering. I will not deny it is hard work and takes much effort, and without doubt, the benefits are worth their weight in gold.

What brings me the most joy in life is helping others. To know I am making a difference in the world. To inspire people on the path of healing and for all beings to realize they are worthy and deserving of liberation. This journey is for any seeker looking to combat stress, anxiety, pain and suffering, and to lay down the foundation to knowing the True Self.

So glad you are here. Let us begin.

WRITE, DRAW, DOODLE, EXPRESS

Day 1

Welcome to your Joy Journey. Take a few moments to reflect on where you are in your life at this moment. What is it that you most love about yourself and your life? What is it that you most want to achieve on this journey? What do you feel your purpose is in this moment, in this lifetime?**

What brings you Joy today?

WRITE, DRAW, DOODLE, EXPRESS

Day 2

What are a few thoughts and actions you have which you feel do not serve you? What are the Seeds you will plant today and watch them grow on the course of this journey?

What brings you Joy today?

WRITE, DRAW, DOODLE, EXPRESS

Write your limitations in the circle

Write your advantages outside the circle

Day 3

What is your experience of your breathing exercises? Do you find your exhalation is as deep as your inhalations? What conceptions do you have of yourself which may be limiting? How might you change your perspective from limitation to possibility?

What brings you Joy today?

WRITE, DRAW, DOODLE, EXPRESS

Day 4

What are you learning about the way you have been breathing all your life? Write yourself some affirmations of encouragement. How do the breathing techniques make you feel?

What brings you Joy today?

WRITE, DRAW, DOODLE, EXPRESS

Day 5

Where in your life do you see your Ego acting out the strongest?
In which of your relationships might you feel it would be helpful to practice
non-reactivity? When you practice this, how does it make you feel?

What brings you Joy today?

WRITE, DRAW, DOODLE, EXPRESS

Day 6

List the areas in your body where you felt sensations during the body scan and the places where you felt tiny or no feelings at all. Revisit this exercise at the end of your journey, and note any changes.

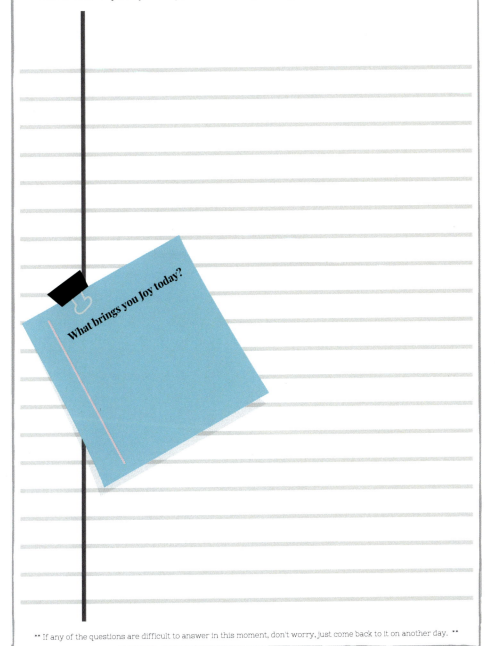

What brings you Joy today?

WRITE, DRAW, DOODLE, EXPRESS

Dear Journal;

What brings you Joy today?

Day 7

Set a timer for 2 min. Do a stream of consciousness writing on what is present for you in this very moment. Meaning you write down whatever comes, without stopping, rephrasing, contemplating or judging. The idea here is just to let your thoughts flow as you write. After 2 mins is up, you can journal about your insights if you so wish.

Ready, Set, Go!

END OF WEEK ONE

You have completed seven days, and you have just 21 more to go!

I want to offer some tips and suggestions to help make your experience strong.

Practice space:
Set up a place to return to each day. Make it sacred and inviting. For example, I have a room designated for my practice in my home and office. In it, I have my meditation cushion, my yoga mat, a shawl or blanket and any props I may need to assist me in my posture. I also have an altar where I display a few small things that inspire me, such as pictures of my teachers, incense, some sacred books, a statue of the Buddha and candles. In this way, each time you return to sit, you are welcomed by the energy you are creating by your practice.

Time to Practice:
Morning traditionally is considered the best time to practice. Early enough when your household is not yet up, and the business of the day has yet to capture you. It also supports the idea of waking up rather than sleepiness which a practice before bed may do. However, you may be finding it challenging " finding the time" to fit your training into your already busy life. Therefore, I suggest setting your morning alarm 30 minutes earlier or sitting right after work before getting dinner ready. Remember, the ego-mind will not like attempting to tame it. It will put up every excuse and obstacle possible to sway you, which is why a daily practice is imperative to create this excellent and healthy practice each and every day.

Position:
Meditation and proper breathing techniques are about waking up, energizing and building life force. This is why we sit upright, with a straight spine, not reclined or lying down. Sure, some practices encourage lying down, such as body-scan meditation. However, if you cannot sit on a cushion on the floor, then use a chair. On my website in the library, I have a short video showing how to use a meditation cushion properly. Check it out www.andid.ca.

Breathwork:
The breathing exercises you are doing each day may be challenging to start. In my experience, most people do not breathe properly. They tend to breathe very shallowly, using only the upper portion of their lungs. Go back to the instructional video and follow along carefully if this is you. If you still have issues, reach out to me personally by booking a soul coaching session.

Support:
The Joy Network is a place for you to ask questions and share your experiences with other Joy Seekers. If you are not yet a member, join today on Facebook.

Gratitude is such
a wonderful way of
opening the heart to joy.
What are you
grateful for today?

Muladhara - Red

Day 8

When you focus on the root chakra, can you feel sensations at the base of your spine? If yes, please describe them. (**refer to glossary)
What elements of your family bring you courage and strength?
How might your past be causing you feelings of fear or restriction?

What brings you Joy today?

Svadhisthana - Orange

Day 9

When you focus on the second chakra, can you feel sensations in the sacral and pelvic region? If yes, please describe them. For example, what brings you pleasure in your life now? What brought you joy in your life when you were a child? Whom might you like to have a more intimate connection to in your life?

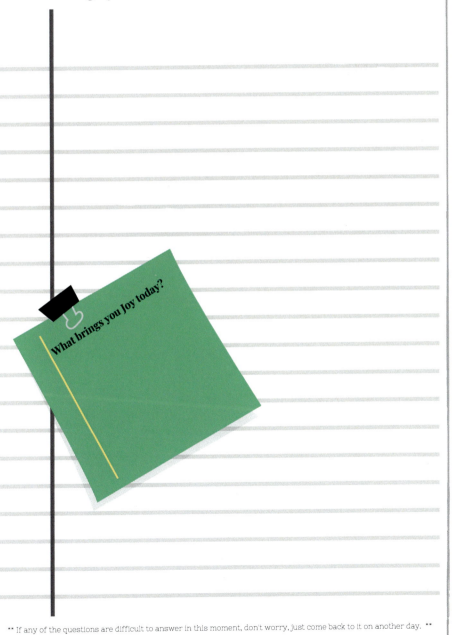

What brings you Joy today?

Manipura – Yellow

Day 10

When you focus on the third chakra, are you able to feel sensations in your solar plexus? If yes, please describe them. When are you the most confident and self-assured In your life,? What do you think your purpose is in this lifetime? How are you fulfilling this purpose, or what might be holding you back?

What brings you Joy today?

Anahata - Green

Day 11

When you focus on the fourth chakra, are you able to feel sensations in your heart? If yes, please describe them. What brings love and joy to your life? What thoughts do you have about yourself that might be causing you to feel stuck, beaten or hurt? What will you do to change this internal dialogue, and what will you now forgive yourself for?

What brings you Joy today?

Vishuddha - Light Blue

Day 12

When you focus on the fifth chakra, are you able to feel sensations in your throat? If yes, please describe them. What do you wish you could say out loud to yourself or someone else? What negative thoughts do you feed that do not serve you, and what new ideas will you now offer yourself?

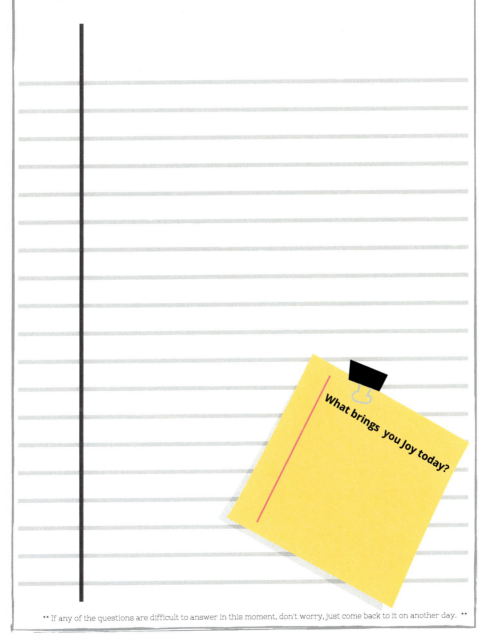

What brings you Joy today?

Ajna - Indigo

Day 13

When you focus on the sixth chakra, can you feel sensations in the space between your eyes? If yes, please describe them.

What do you sense you are most intuitive about? How do you think your ego is causing you to be stuck in destructive thought patterns? What negative thoughts and actions do you want to let go of and what positive habits will take their place?

What brings you joy today?

Sahasrara – Violet

Day 14

When you focus on the seventh chakra, can you feel sensations at the crown of your head? If yes, please describe them. Are you able to rest in the pure awareness of all that is? Are you able to feel a connection to Source? If not, what might be holding you back, and what might you like to work on to connect in this way?

Remember not to judge.
This is a process.
Be easy, be kind
You can always
return here again
and again

What brings you Joy today?

** If any of the questions are difficult to answer in this moment, don't worry, just come back to it on another day. **

In moments of doubt,
anger or frustration,
take a moment to
pause, breathe, and
know that Joy
has got your back.

END OF WEEK TWO

You have completed 14 days, and you have just 14 more to go!

At this point on your journey, you must be feeling a new level of energy and awareness. Excellent, this is what I intended!

Over the week, I have asked you some pretty in-depth questions about how you feel in particular areas of your body and any sensations that live there. If you have not taken time in your life to make inquiries in this way before, perhaps you are feeling a bit stumped? I suggest that you study the glossary of terms at the end of this journal for suggestions on connecting to these sensations.

Even with these word prompts, you still may come up blank. You may experience sensations in some parts of your body and none in others areas. What I know for sure is that the body never lies. What you may think of as "nothing" is really "something"; the area could be blocked, guarded, or shut down. All of this is essential information.

Our bodies may shut down because the mind is dealing with trauma or remorse over something we may have done or something which may have been done to us. Emotional wounds get locked up in the body and form cysts that contain all our sorrows. Working with the energy centres of our bodies, we are also working with the consciousness of our tissues. Every experience we have in our life from conception to this moment lives in the membranes of our being.

If you suspect that one or more of your chakra centres are blocked or too open, practice the meditation again provided in the Joy Journey to help bring balance.

Day 15

What impressed you the most about how Siddhartha became the Buddha? What do you notice that you cling to in your life and on this journey? What do you see that you have an aversion to in your life and on this journey?

What brings you joy today?

WRITE, DRAW, DOODLE, EXPRESS

Day 16

Did you feel sensations during your Ana Pana practice? First, jot down some of the feelings and sensations you felt (*refer to the glossary). Then, write about the changes you are noticing in your day-to-day activities. What is the voice in your head telling you about yourself?
How are you responding to challenging situations as they arise?

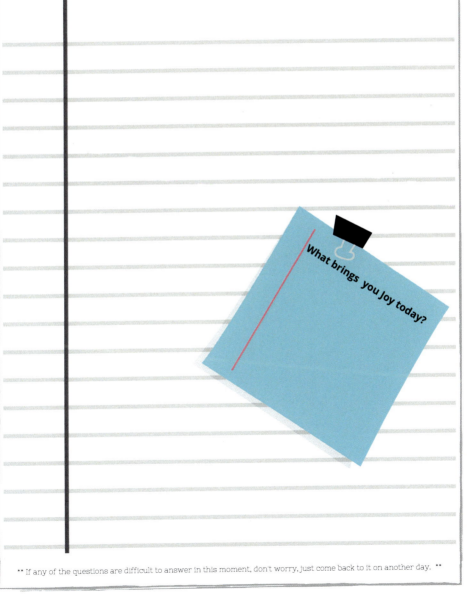

What brings you Joy today?

WRITE, DRAW, DOODLE, EXPRESS

Day 17

How does your life bring you peace and harmony? Are you noticing any changes in how you react to stressful situations? The video tells us that meditation and mindfulness exercises help shrink the area of the brain called the amygdala. Knowing that you have the power to pause before a knee-jerk reaction, list some examples where this will help you.

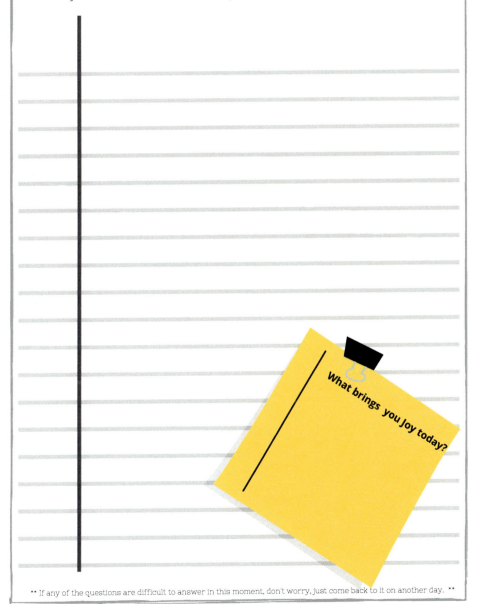

What brings you joy today?

WRITE, DRAW, DOODLE, EXPRESS

Day 18

In your practice today what state did you find yourself in the most? Pain, emotion, wandering mind? Explain your understanding of how to deal with these states as they arise and fall away. Finally, write down the benefits you are noticing in your journey thus far.

What brings you joy today?

WRITE, DRAW, DOODLE, EXPRESS

Day 19

Knowing that the brain has the ability to change and grow new neurons what are some areas in your life would you like to focus on changing from the current states you find yourself in?
How might this help in dealing with the pain and discomfort that you experience on a daily level?

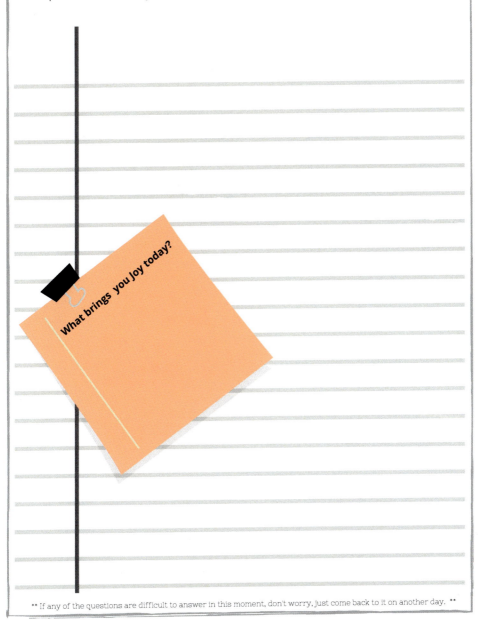

What brings you joy today?

WRITE, DRAW, DOODLE, EXPRESS

Day 20

What emotions were most present for you in your practice today? Where did they land in your body? What sensations came into your awareness with these feeling states? How does your understanding offer you a new perspective in dealing with feeling states as they arise?

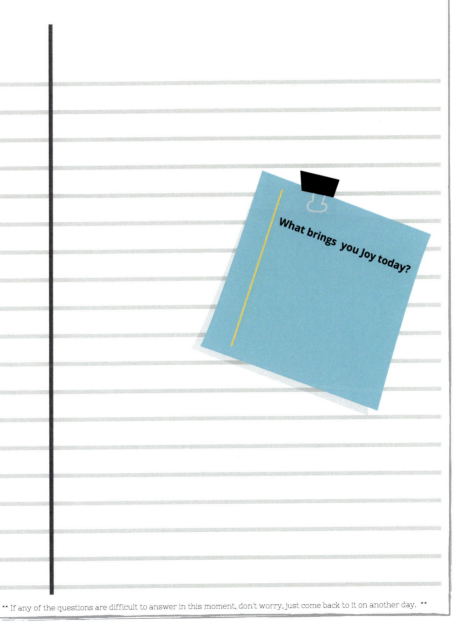

What brings you joy today?

Even in the darkest corners
of our hearts, where shame,
blame and judgment lie,
the power of Joy can still
shine through.

END OF WEEK THREE

You have completed 21 days; you have just seven more to go!

This week we took a deeper dive into the teachings of formal practice. Developing tools to encourage simply "being" without "reacting." No easy task, to be sure!

As the saying goes, neurons that fire together wire together. Even if that synaptic pattern does not serve us, or causes us to be in states of discomfort, the brain does not make this distinction. If you are wired in believing you are a failure, your brain will support you in that thinking.

The Buddha so nobly taught in the first of his four noble truths that human suffering is inevitable. We can not escape it; pain, desire, attachment, aversion, are all a part of what it means to be human. But, while we may not be able to escape it, we can most certainly learn to tame it.

One of the most significant challenges of meditation practice is training the mind. The mind is like a wild animal, constantly out on the prowl looking for its next battle or feed. Taming the beast is no easy task, and it often causes many folks to give up. "Oh, it's too hard, my mind is too busy, I have so many things to get done, I can not stay still."

I understand these mind states; why would the ego want the "True Self" to take control? The ego wants what the ego wants, and a sharp mind, able to cut through doubt and lethargy, is undoubtedly not one of them.

The ego wants to stay in control, binding us to our senses, convincing us we need the ego to survive. Society plays on the ego by bombarding us with notions on what constitutes success, beauty, wealth, all of which take us out of the present moment and into states of desire or lack. No wonder we suffer so, no wonder we doubt our abilities to change. This is a dull and untrained mind.

Science tells us that neuroplasticity is possible and proven. We can rewire our thoughts and reactions in ways that serve us better. It takes courage to change, courage to face ourselves, courage to be truthful, and courage to be humble. Diligence, consistency, commitment and time are the remedies. Anyone can do it with proper training and proper support. We can sharpen the mind to cut through that which causes suffering.
We can know Joy every day.

WRITE, DRAW, DOODLE, EXPRESS

Day 21

What practice did you choose to do today? Why did you choose it? How was it different from the first time you practiced it?

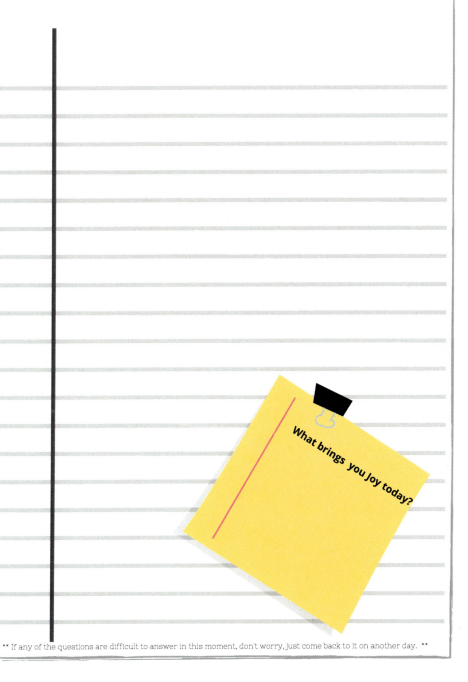

What brings you Joy today?

WRITE, DRAW, DOODLE, EXPRESS

Day 22

What impressed you most from the story called "swimology?"
In the Metta practice, were you able to send love to the people you
envisioned; on your left and right side? How do you feel about sending
kindness, caring, and well-wishes to all the people you brought to mind?
Are you able to offer yourself this same kindness and love that you
provided to others? If you are struggling with this, take a few moments
to write down some reasons why.**

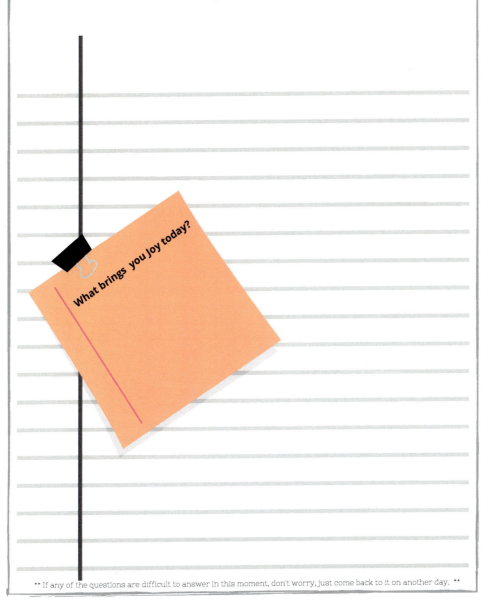

What brings you joy today?

WRITE, DRAW, DOODLE, EXPRESS

Day 23

Who in your life do you wish to offer your forgiveness to, and for what? Who do you now forgive, and for what? Who are the people that you still struggle to forgive? What might be holding you back? What deeds, actions, or thoughts do you wish to forgive yourself?

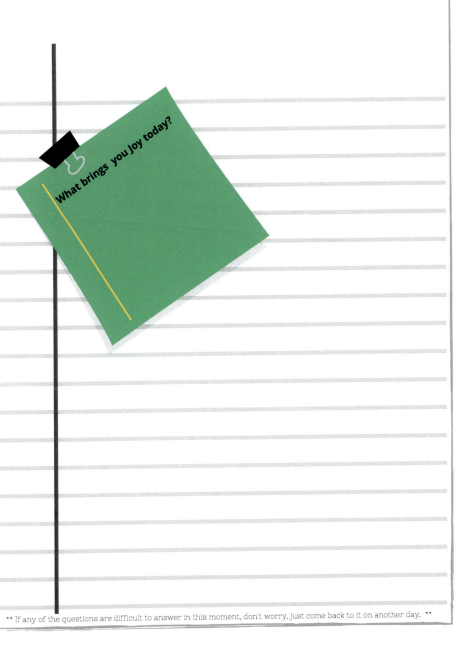

What brings you joy today?

WRITE, DRAW, DOODLE, EXPRESS

Day 24

Who or what did you find relatively easy to offer Tonglen practise? What situations or persons, including yourself, is Tonglen more challenging? What is it you may still be holding on to? What might you think is the underlying issue at hand? Remember, take time with this practice, don't force the letting go or the opening up. Tonglen is a technique to be practiced repeatedly. Returning to those states that may be difficult at this moment becomes more manageable as time moves forward.

What brings you joy today?

WRITE, DRAW, DOODLE, EXPRESS

Day 25

What issue or memory came to mind with your practice of R.A.I.N.?
What did you recognize in your awareness - feelings, emotions,
judgments? Were you able to be with those states, and what came up as
you opened your attention to these states? Then, when you investigated
further, what did you notice, and how did it help you neutralize or come
back to a natural state with that awareness and acceptance?

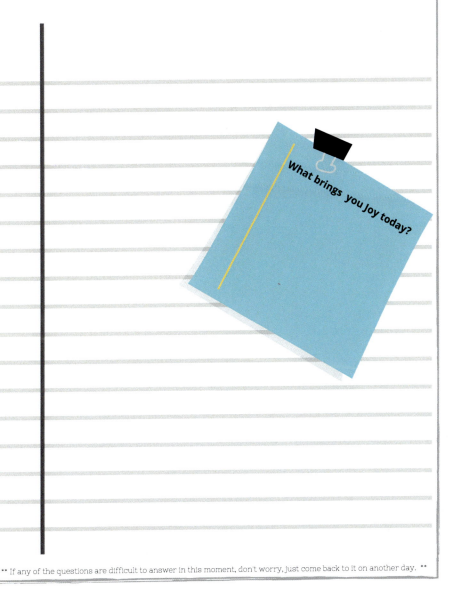

What brings you Joy today?

WRITE, DRAW, DOODLE, EXPRESS

Day 26

Make a list of thoughts, deeds, actions, and beliefs that may cause harm to you or others. Then, use this list to practice Ho'opnopono as you move forward on your journey.

What brings you joy today?

WRITE, DRAW, DOODLE, EXPRESS

Day 27

Has this journey helped you to become more courageous? If yes, write about it. What layers of fear still reside in you, and how will you use all the skills you acquired on this journey to help you move through and beyond?

What brings you Joy today?

WRITE, DRAW, DOODLE, EXPRESS

Day 28

Congratulations. You did it! What an incredible accomplishment. Finding Joy in life does not mean we have to be smiling and happy every day. Joy is about connection, about being in the moment, about loving yourself in all states of being. It is about infusing even just one joyful ray of light in each day. Take some time to review your whole journey. How have you grown, changed, advanced from where you were on day one to where you are now?

What brings you Joy today?

END OF WEEK FOUR

You have completed 28 days, now what?

First I say celebrate! You deserve a lot of credit to have completed this challenging journey. Some of the questions I asked along the way required honesty and courage. The reflections and insights you made are yours to keep and return to in time of need and encouragement. Yay!

It takes 21 days to form a habit, and now you have created one. As you continue, I assure you it will be the most rewarding and insightful habit of your life. The Joy Journey intends to lay down the foundation of a daily practice. To offer you first-hand experience of how it feels to follow the path and know more Joy.

As human beings, we have an immense capacity for compassion and love. We can connect with the "Source" of all things. (insert whatever name fills your heart, be it God, Divine, Jesus, Moon, Mohamad, Spirit, Universe.) We are energetic beings that can vibrate at the same frequency as this pure potential. Often thought of as the return home, if you will.

The pranayama exercises we did every day for the last 28 days are a prime example of how this energy feels and how we can ignite it when we feel low or depleted. We also worked with the chakra centres in our bodies to awaken and raise our life force energy further. These are tools you now have access to any time anywhere. To me, this is Joy!

My suggestion for you now is that you keep on practicing. Everyday! Devote at least 30 minutes to your practice. Longer when possible. If you miss a day, be kind to yourself and start again. Treat every sitting as an opportunity to better your craft. To be more compassionate, humble, and cherish your life force. The Buddha taught his disciples always to maintain a beginner's mind. Stay curious, steadfast, genuine. Never assume that the teachings of a spiritual warrior are ever over.

Start this journey again if you like. Take other challenges that are out there. Follow some of our great teachers and guides. Study! Take classes and workshops. Join a meditation group in your local area. Form a group of your own with other friends who may like to sit together. Go on retreat!

I love getting emails and messages from other Joy Seekers, so stay in touch. Join the Joy Network support page. Share some of your experiences. Ask questions, get support, offer support, start discussions. Follow me at https://www.facebook.com/groups/thejoynetwork, or www.andid.ca, where I offer tips, insights, resources, classes and workshops.

It has been such an honour and privilege to guide you on this journey. Thank you for allowing me to share my passion with you. If you have feedback, I welcome it. You can reach me at andidrmt@andid.ca

Go forth and live your Joy!

In peace and friendship;
Andi D.

Always remember
what you feed
grows stronger,
and neurons that
fire together,
wire together

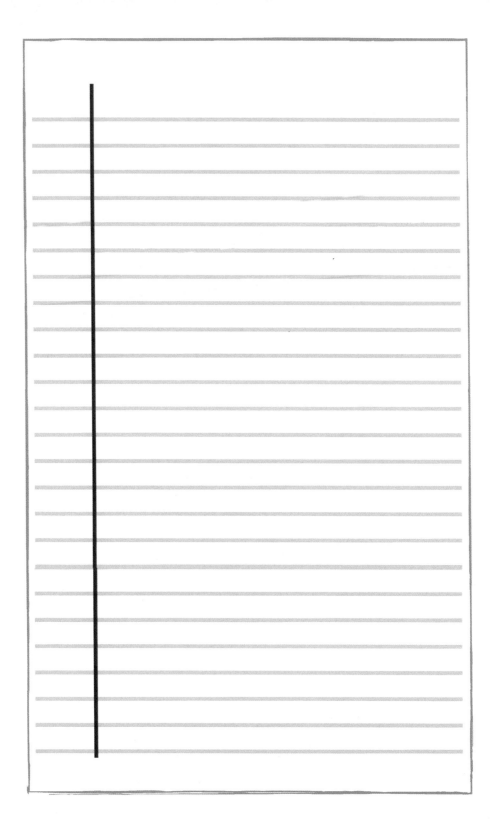

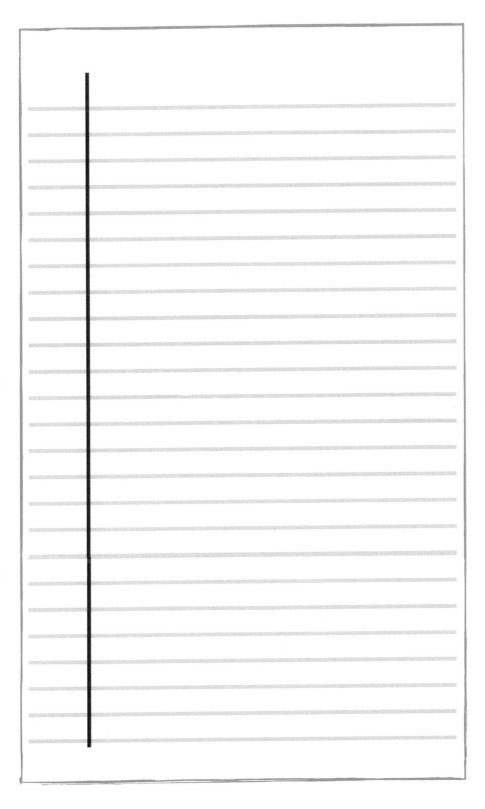

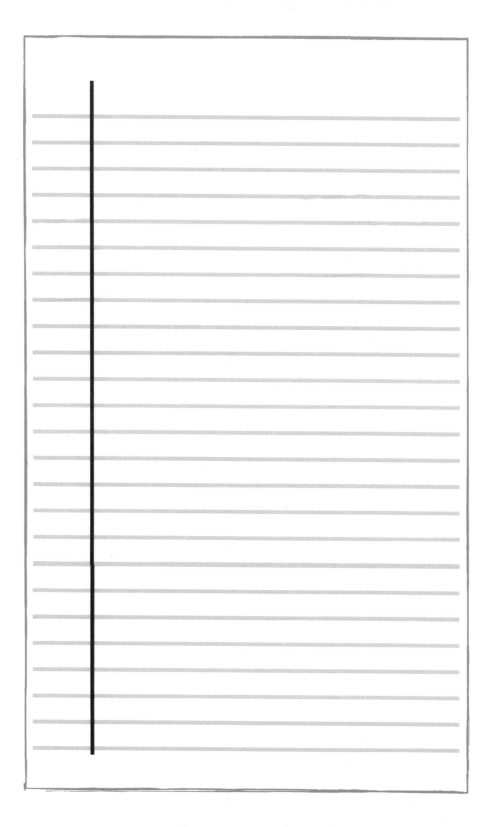

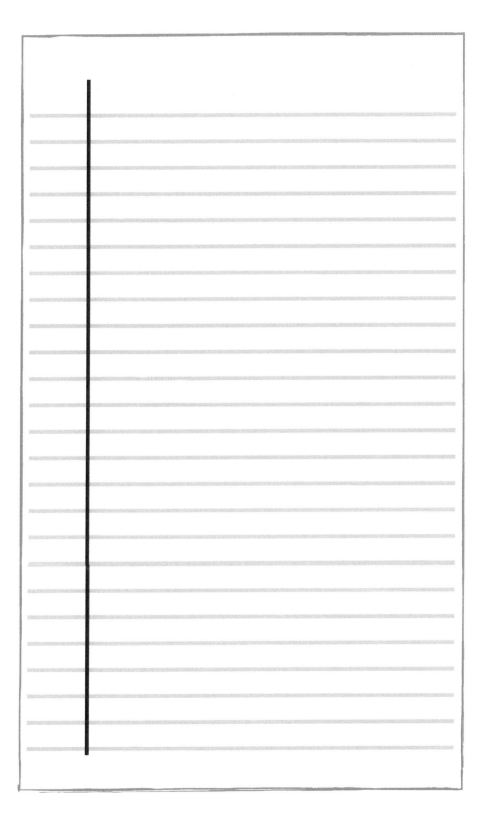

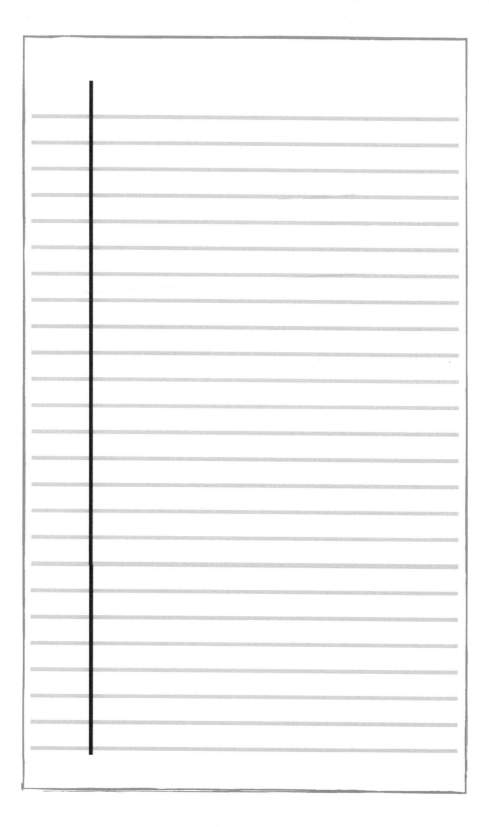

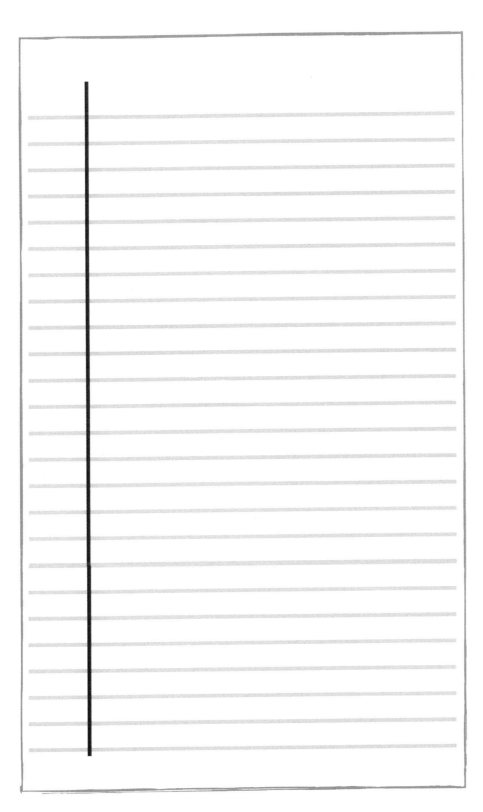

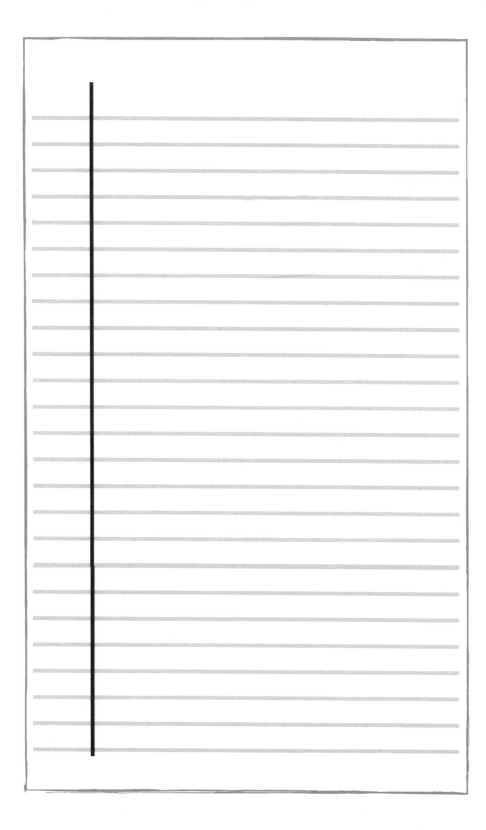

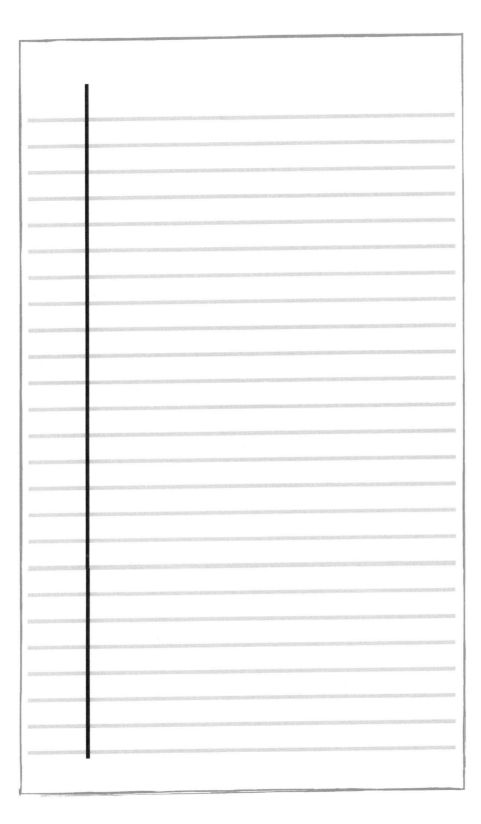

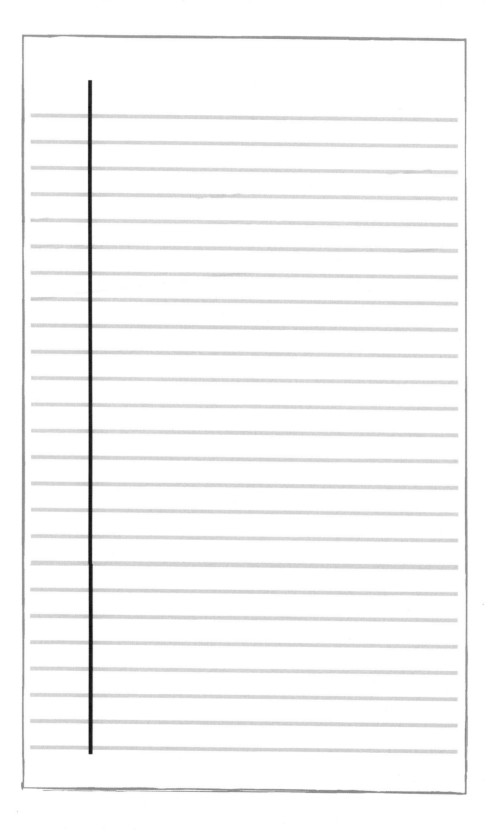

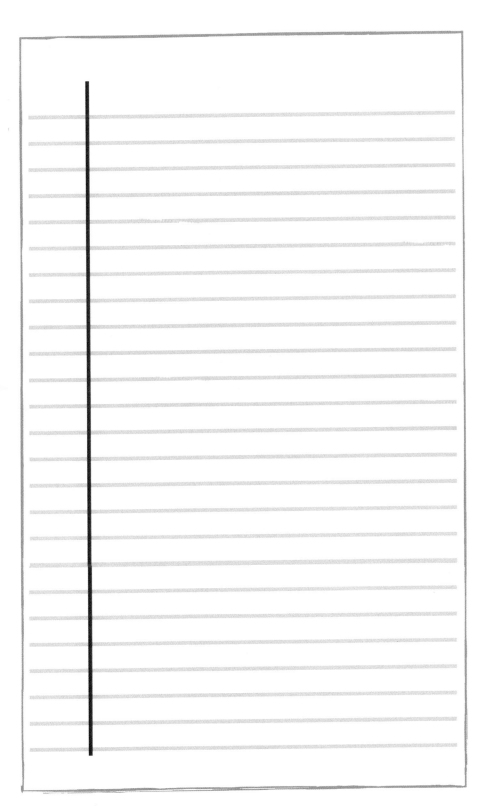

Glossary of Sensations

Achy
Airy
Blocked
Breathless
Bruised
Burning
Buzzy
Clammy
Clenched
Cold
Constricted
Contained
Contracted
Dizzy
Drained
Dull
Electric
Empty
Expanded
Flowing
Fluid
Fluttery
Frozen
Full
Gentle

Hard
Heavy
Hollow
Hot
Icy
Itchy
Jumpy
Knotted
Light
Loose
Nauseous
Numb
Pain
Pounding
Prickly
Pulsing
Queasy
Radiating
Relaxed
Releasing
Rigid
Sensitive
Settled
Shaky
Shivery

Slow
Smooth
Soft
Sore
Spacey
Spacious
Sparkly
Stiff
Still
Suffocated
Sweaty
Tender
Tense
Throbbing
Tight
Tingling
Trembly
Twitchy
Vibrating
Warm
Wobbly
Woodency

Glossary of Feelings

Accepting / Open
Calm
Centered
Content
Fulfilled
Patient
Peaceful
Present
Relaxed
Serene
Trusting
Safe
Warm
Worthy
Curious
Engaged
Exploring
Fascinated
Interested
Intrigued
Involved
Stimulated

Aliveness / Joy
Amazed
Awe
Bliss
Delighted
Eager
Ecstatic
Enchanted
Energized
Engaged
Enthusiastic
Excited
Free
Happy
Inspired
Invigorated
Lively
Playful
Radiant
Refreshed
Rejuvenated
Renewed
Satisfied
Thrilled
Vibrant

Angry / Annoyed
Agitated
Aggravated
Bitter
Contempt
Cynical
Disdain
Disgruntled
Disturbed
Edgy
Exasperated
Frustrated
Furious
Grouchy
Hostile
Impatient
Irritated
Irate
Moody
On edge
Outraged
Pissed
Resentful
Upset
Vindictive

Courageous / Powerful
Adventurous
Brave
Capable
Confident
Daring
Determined
Free
Grounded
Proud
Strong
Worthy
Valiant

Connected / Loving
Accepting
Affectionate
Caring
Compassion
Empathy
Fulfilled
Present

Despair / Sad
Anguish
Depressed
Despondent
Disappointed
Discouraged
Forlorn
Gloomy
Grief
Heartbroken
Hopeless
Lonely
Longing
Melancholy
Sorrow
Teary
Unhappy
Upset
Weary
Yearning

Embarrassed / Shame
Ashamed
Humiliated
Inhibited
Mortified
Self-conscious
Useless
Weak
Worthless

Fear
Afraid
Anxious
Apprehensive
Frightened
Hesitant
Nervous
Panic
Paralyzed
Scared
Terrified
Worried
Fragile
Helpless
Sensitive

Guilt
Regret
Remorseful
Sorry

Hopeful
Encouraged
Expectant
Optimistic
Trusting

Powerless
Impotent
Incapable
Resigned
Trapped
Victim

Tender
Calm
Caring
Loving
Reflective
Self-loving
Serene
Vulnerable
Warm

Disconnected/Numb
Aloof
Bored
Confused
Distant
Empty
Indifferent
Isolated
Lethargic
Listless
Removed
Resistant
Shut Down
Uneasy
Withdrawn

Grateful
Appreciative
Blessed
Delighted
Fortunate
Grace
Humbled
Lucky
Moved
Thankful
Touched

Stressed / Tense	Unsettled / Doubt
Anxious	Apprehensive
Burned out	Concerned
Cranky	Dissatisfied
Depleted	Disturbed
Edgy	Grouchy
Exhausted	Hesitant
Frazzled	Inhibited
Overwhelm	Perplexed
Rattled	Questioning
Rejecting	Rejecting
Restless	Reluctant
Shaken	Shocked
Tight	Skeptical
Weary	Suspicious
Worn out	Ungrounded
	Unsure
	Worried

Manufactured by Amazon.ca
Bolton, ON

34656702R00052